Down on the Farm

CHICKENS

Hannah Ray

QEB Publishing, Inc

QEB

First published in the United States in 2006 by
QEB Publishing, Inc.
23062 La Cadena Drive
Laguna Hills, CA 92653
www.qeb-publishing.com

Library of Congress Control Number: 2005910914

ISBN 978-1-59566-183-8

Written by Hannah Ray
Designed by Liz Wiffen
Consultant Sally Morgan
Editor Paul Manning
Picture Researcher Joanne Forrest Smith
Illustrations by Chris Davidson

Publisher Steve Evans
Editorial Director Jean Coppendale
Art Director Zeta Davies

Printed and bound in China

Picture credits

Key: t = top, b = bottom, c = center,
l = left, r = right, FC = front cover

Alamy /James Clarke Images 12T, /Image State 4BC,
/Worldwide Picture Library 10; **Corbis** /Craig Aurness
18, /W Perry Conway 16T, /Ashley Cooper 8T, /Robert
Dowling FC & 1, 16B, 17T&B, /Larry Downing/Reuters
19T, /Macduff Everton 13, /Rick Gomez 15, /Philip
Gould 19CR, /David Thomas 14TR; **Getty Images**
/Jane Burton 22, /Tim Flach 9, /Klaus Hackenberg
14TL, /GK & Vikki Hart 6, /Tony Page 5, /Pier 4,
/Henry Wolf 12B; **Still Pictures**/Ullstein bid/KPA 11.

CONTENTS

Words in **bold** can be found in the Glossary on page 22.

Chickens on the farm

Do you know where we get eggs for breakfast, and the tender meat that tastes so good in salads, sandwiches, and at picnics?

Both of these types of foods come from chickens.

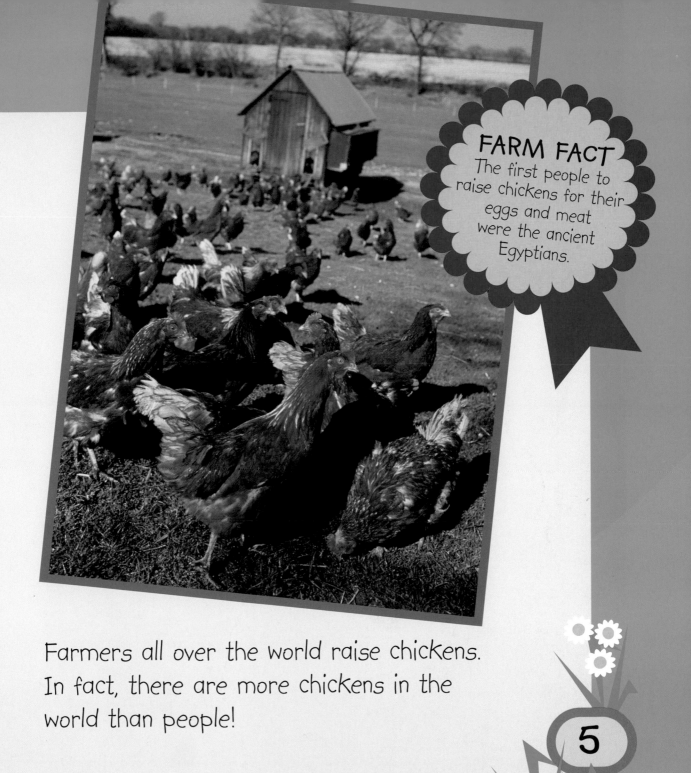

FARM FACT
The first people to raise chickens for their eggs and meat were the ancient Egyptians.

Farmers all over the world raise chickens. In fact, there are more chickens in the world than people!

Chickens from beak to tail

A full-grown chicken is about 15 in. (40 cm) tall and weighs around 6 lbs. (3 kg)—the same as three bags of flour.

Eye

Wing

Beak
(chickens
do not have
any teeth)

Feet

Comb

Wattle

Height of
six-year-old child

FARM FACT
Chickens have wings
but they can only fly
short distances. The
longest recorded flight
by a chicken is
13 seconds.

Height of
chicken

Male chickens, called
roosters, have a
wattle and a **comb**.
Roosters have more
colorful **plumage** than
female chickens.

7

It's a chicken's life...

A **chick** starts life as an egg inside its mother. After the egg has been laid, the mother chicken, or hen, sits on it to keep it warm and turns it over and over.

After 21 days, the chick uses a special egg tooth on its beak to chip its way out of the egg.

8

FARM FACT
A hen clucks to her chick while it is still inside the egg.

Newborn chicks have soft, fluffy feathers. After eight days, other feathers start to grow.

After two months, the chick has most of its grown-up feathers. By four and a half months, the chick is fully grown. A female chicken is now old enough to lay her own eggs.

Most chickens live for about seven years.

Who rules the roost?

In a henhouse, some hens are more important than others. This special order of importance is called a pecking order, because the hens peck and bully one another to find out who is boss!

Bigger, stronger hens take the highest **perches** in the henhouse. The chickens that are lower down the pecking order stay away from the bigger chickens and hold their heads low.

Egg-citing!

Different types of chickens lay different-colored eggs. Most hens lay eggs with white or brown shells, but some hens' eggs are pink, blue, or even green.

An egg yolk

The color of the **yolk** depends on what the hen has been eating. Hens that eat lots of grass and vegetables lay eggs with rich orange-yellow yolks.

Free-range eggs come from chickens that are free to wander outside.

You can tell if an egg is fresh by placing it in a bowl of water. If the egg is fresh, it will sink. If the egg is old, it will float.

Eggs, meat, and feathers

Farmers raise chickens for their meat as well as their eggs. Chickens that give us eggs are called laying hens. Chickens raised for meat are called broilers.

FARM FACT
Soon, chicken feathers might be used for the padding in diapers and to mop up oil spills!

Scientists have found out that parts of a chicken's feathers are very absorbent. This means they are good at soaking up liquid.

Feathered friends

PRAIRIE CHICKEN
These chickens are from North America. The males have a special orange patch on their necks which they puff up to attract female chickens.

POLISH BANTAM
Famous for their amazing feathers, these small chickens come from Poland. Some of them even have beards, too!

16

FARM FACT
Chickens make great alarm clocks! Farmers today still wake up to the sound of roosters crowing.

FRIZZLE

Frizzle chickens are easy to spot. Their feathers curl back toward their heads, rather than lying flat and pointing toward their tails.

RED JUNGLE FOWL

This chicken lives in Asia and eats seeds, fruit, and insects. The Red Jungle Fowl is the chicken that all other chickens came from.

17

Chickens around the world

UKRAINE

Decorating hens' eggs for Easter is a tradition in many countries. An Easter egg from Ukraine is called a "pysanka." The beautiful pictures and patterns on these eggs mean different things, from happiness to good luck.

CHINA

In China, each year is named after one of twelve animals. People born in the Chinese Year of the Rooster are hard-working and brave.

18

FARM FACT
Chickens are braver than people think. Chickens that are kept as household pets soon learn to stand up to cats and dogs.

Egg racing with hand-painted eggs on the White House lawn.

THE UNITED STATES

Every year an Easter Egg Roll takes place on the lawn of the White House in Washington, DC, home of the U.S. President. The Easter Egg Roll was started in 1878 and still happens every year.

Make your own chirpy chicks

Have fun making a box of chirpy chicks!
All you need is a carton of six eggs, a
pin, a bowl, and some paints.

1 Ask a grown-
up to use a pin to
make a hole at the
top and bottom of
a raw egg.

2 Hold the egg over
a bowl and blow into
the hole at the top.
If you blow hard, the
yolk and white will
come out of the hole
at the bottom.

3 Hold the eggshell under the faucet and run water through it to clean it out.

BRIGHT IDEA
Ask a grown-up to help you use the leftover egg whites and yolks to make a cake.

4 Paint your blown egg to look like a little chick.

5 Blow the other eggs and paint them until you have a set of chirpy chicks! Try adding googly eyes or fluffy feathers (you can buy these from a craft store) and stick them on with glue.

Glossary and Index

chick   baby chicken

comb   a flap of skin on the top of a rooster's head

perch   where a chicken sits, rests, and sleeps

plumage   feathers on a chicken

tradition   something that is passed on from parents to their children, and then on to their children

wattle   flap of skin hanging from the neck of a bird

yolk   yellow part in the middle of a hen's egg

22

Ideas for teachers and parents

- Research pictures of different *breeds* of chickens and use them to make a poster. You could make factsheets comparing the children's favorite *breeds*.

- Look at pictures of hens and roosters of the same *breed*. How do they differ?

- Take a clean plastic yogurt container or small margarine tub. Thread a needle with thread or string and carefully push it through the *base* of the container. Tie a knot in the end of the thread. Tug on the thread to make a clucking sound. Running your fingernail down the thread will produce a longer cluck!

- Make a chicken collage. Draw the outline of a chicken on a large piece of paper. Look through magazines, newspapers, etc., and cut out anything related to chickens, chicks, and eggs. Collect feathers, scraps of material, and other odds and ends. Paste down everything you have collected to fill in the chicken outline.

- Draw a chicken outline on a piece of letter-size paper. Photocopy it a few times and challenge the children to design some funky feathered plumage. Encourage them to *be bold* and wacky and to use bright colors. They could add impressive combs and experiment with different shapes for the feathers.

- Make a word *search* for the children using chicken-related vocabulary from this *book*.

- If possible, visit a children's farm so the children can *see* real chickens.

- *See* how many jokes, stories, poems, and rhymes about chickens the children can think of. Can they make up a chicken poem of their own?